The Kentish Coa
Whitstable to I

The forty-three photographs in this album are from the Keasbury-Gordon Photograph Archive, a unique collection of historical images taken from 'magic lantern' projection slides and early photographs. They capture fleeting moments in the lives of ordinary people in Whitstable, Herne Bay, Margate, Ramsgate, Dover, Folkestone, Hythe and elsewhere .... in streets and harbours and on the beach, mostly between the 1890s and 1930s. There is also a fascinating 1840s map of Kent.

I hope you enjoy these rarely seen views of the Kentish coast.

Andrew Gill

Whitstable

Whitstable fishermen

West Beach, Whitstable

Herne Bay Clock Tower

Herne Bay High Street

Herne Bay Beach

Cycle racing, Herne Bay

Pierrots on the beach, Margate

Margate Harbour

Marine Terrace, Margate

Marine Terrace, Margate

Queen's Parade, Margate

Margate Beach

Margate

The Camera Obscura, Margate

Margate Lifeboat

Margate Pier

Pierrots on the beach, Margate

Perkins' Bathing Machines, Margate

Broadstairs

Ramsgate Harbour

New Road, Ramsgate

Circus procession in Ramsgate in 1899

Circus procession in Ramsgate in 1899

Circus procession in Ramsgate in 1899

Pleasure boats, Ramsgate

Ramsgate Quayside

Ramsgate

Kingsdown

The Beach and Castle, Dover

East Cliff, Dover

Dover

Dover Harbour

The 'Boulogne' Boat, Folkestone

Fishmarket, Folkestone

Victoria Pier, Folkestone

Folkestone Harbour

Folkestone Harbour

A pleasure boat, Folkestone

High Street, Folkestone

High Street, Hythe

High Street, Hythe

Hythe

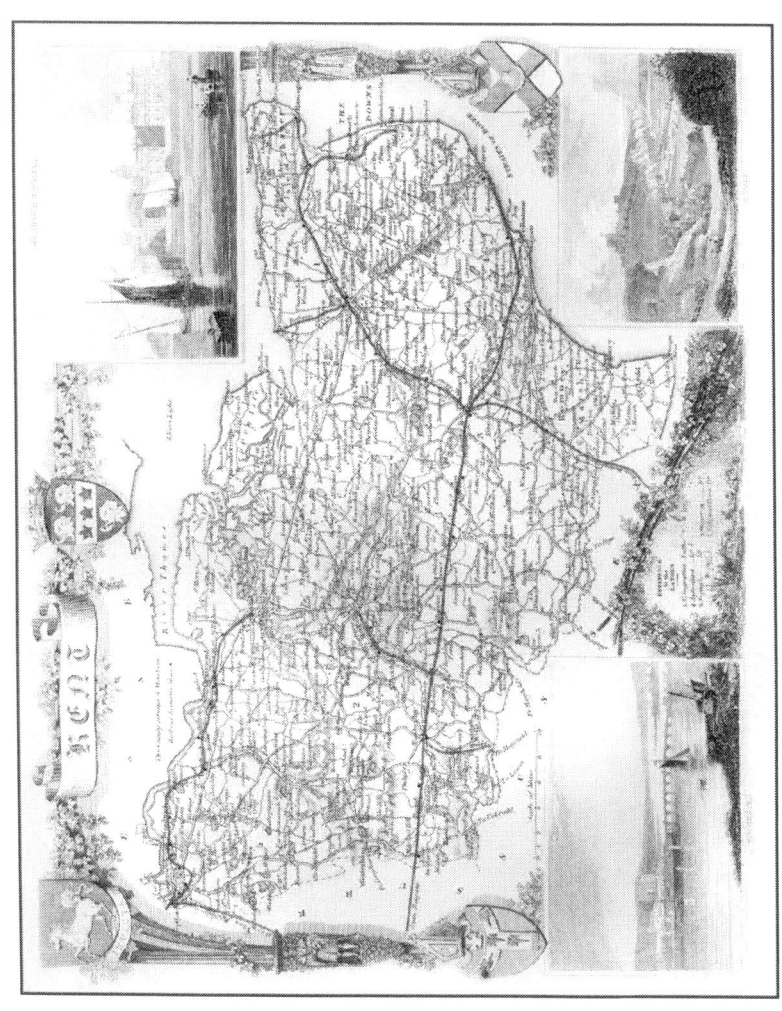

Kent in the 1840s

The Magic Lantern

The magic lantern was the predecessor of the pre-digital slide projector. The first magic lanterns were made in the mid-1600s by natural philosophers (early scientists) who were exploring the nature and commercial potential of optics. Light sources and lenses improved throughout the 1700s and 1800s and as a consequence, it was possible to show bigger, brighter and clearer pictures to ever larger audiences. During Queen Victoria's reign, magic lantern shows became established as mass-media entertainment. Shows could be lavish, theatrical events with all the razzmatazz of today's TV talent contests, with multiple lanterns to produce special effects. Magic lanterns were also used in Church and village halls and educational establishments for talks and lectures and, of course, in ordinary homes for family entertainment.

Some slides gave the illusion of movement. These included colourful kaleidoscopes, children skipping, a dentist pulling teeth and a man swallowing rats as he sleeps with his mouth open ...... still a favourite with children (of all ages) who attend my magic lantern shows! At the white-knuckle end of the market, magic lanterns were used to create phantasmagoria horror shows, where terrifying devils, witches and the grim reaper were conjured out of thin air, with accompanying sound effects, in suitably scary venues. These shows employed the latest technology and created sophisticated illusions to entice customers to part with their money and be scared out of their wits.

Magic lantern slides were made of glass. Early ones were hand painted and expensive to produce and buy but, from the mid-1800s, photographic images were applied to slides, mass-production followed and the magic lantern industry boomed. In its heyday, the 1890s, millions of slides were made, particularly in Britain, France and America, for entertainment, amusement, education, spiritual enlightenment and moral crusades.

In Britain, lantern slides could be purchased or hired by mail-order direct from the manufacturers or from local, high-street outlets. Photographic slides produced by the best Victorian photographers, such as those reproduced in this booklet, have pin-sharp clarity and can still make an audience gasp in surprise and delight when shown as part of my Victorian magic lantern shows.

Andrew Gill: I have collected early photographs and optical antiques for over forty years. I am a professional 'magic lantern' showman presenting lantern slide shows and giving talks on Victorian optical entertainments for museums, festivals, special interest groups and universities.

For information about magic lanterns and slides and to contact me, please visit my website **Magic Lantern World** at www.magiclanternist.com

I have published historical booklets and photo albums on the subjects below. They are available from amazon, some as printed books, some as e-books, many in both formats. To see them all and 'look inside', simply search for one of my titles, then click the 'Andrew Gill' link. Alternatively, go to the 'My photo-history booklets' page on my website (see above) and click on the link.

Historical travel guides
Jersey in 1921
Norwich in 1880
Doon the Watter
Liverpool in 1886
Nottingham in 1899
Bournemouth in 1914
Great Yarmouth in 1880
Victorian Walks in Surrey
The Way We Were: Bath
A Victorian Visit to Brighton
A Victorian Visit to Hastings
A Victorian Visit to Falmouth
Newcastle upon Tyne in 1903
Victorian and Edwardian York
The Way We Were: Llandudno
Doncaster: The Way We Were
Victorian and Edwardian Leeds

The Way We Were: Manchester
Victorian and Edwardian Bradford
Victorian and Edwardian Sheffield
A Victorian Visit to Fowey and Looe
A Victorian Visit to Peel, Isle of Man
The Way We Were: The Lake District
Lechlade to Oxford by Canoe in 1875
Guernsey, Sark and Alderney in 1921
East Devon through the Magic Lantern
The River Thames from Source to Sea
North Devon through the Magic Lantern
A Victorian Visit to Ramsey, Isle of Man
A Victorian Visit to Douglas, Isle of Man
Victorian Totnes through the Magic Lantern
Victorian Whitby through the Magic Lantern
Victorian London through the Magic Lantern
St. Ives through the Victorian Magic Lantern
Victorian Torquay through the Magic Lantern
Victorian Glasgow through the Magic Lantern
The Way We Were: Wakefield and Dewsbury
The Way We Were: Hebden Bridge to Halifax
Victorian Edinburgh through the Magic Lantern
Victorian Scarborough through the Magic Lantern
The Way We Were: Hull and the surrounding area
The Way We Were: Harrogate and Knaresborough
A Victorian Tour of North Wales: Rhyl to Llandudno
A Victorian Visit to Lewes and the surrounding area
The Isle of Man through the Victorian Magic Lantern
A Victorian Visit to Helston and the Lizard Peninsula
A Victorian Railway Journey from Plymouth to Padstow
A Victorian Visit to Barmouth and the Surrounding Area
A Victorian Visit to Malton, Pickering and Castle Howard
A Victorian Visit to Eastbourne and the surrounding area
A Victorian Visit to Aberystwyth and the Surrounding Area
A Victorian Visit to Castletown, Port St. Mary and Port Erin
Penzance and Newlyn through the Victorian Magic Lantern
A Victorian Journey to Snowdonia, Caernarfon and Pwllheli
Victorian Brixham and Dartmouth through the Magic Lantern
Victorian Plymouth and Devonport through the Magic Lantern
A Victorian Tour of North Wales: Conwy to Caernarfon via Anglesey
Dawlish, Teignmouth and Newton Abbot through the Victorian Magic Lantern
Staithes, Runswick and Robin Hood's Bay through the Magic Lantern
A Victorian Visit to Cornwall: Morwenstow to Tintagel via Kilkhampton, Bude, Boscastle and Bossiney

Other historical topics
Sarah Jane's Victorian Tour of Scotland
The River Tyne through the Magic Lantern
The 1907 Wrench Cinematograph Catalogue
Victorian Street Life through the Magic Lantern
The First World War through the Magic Lantern
Ballyclare May Fair through the Victorian Magic Lantern
The Story of Burnley's Trams through the Magic Lantern

The Franco-British 'White City' London Exhibition of 1908
The 1907 Wrench 'Optical and Science Lanterns' Catalogue
How They Built the Forth Railway Bridge: A Victorian Magic Lantern Show

Walking Books
Victorian Rossendale Walks
More Victorian Rossendale Walks
Victorian Walks on the Isle of Wight (Book 1)
Victorian Walks on the Isle of Wight (Book 2)
Victorian Rossendale Walks: The End of an Era

Historical photo albums (just photos)
The Way We Were: Suffolk
Norwich: The Way We Were
Sheffield: The Way We Were
The Way We Were: Somerset
Fife through the Magic Lantern
York through the Magic Lantern
Rossendale: The Way We Were
The Way We Were: Lincolnshire
The Way We Were: Cumberland
Burnley through the Magic Lantern
Oban to the Hebrides and St. Kilda
Tasmania through the Magic Lantern
New York through the Magic Lantern
Swaledale through the Magic Lantern
Llandudno through the Magic Lantern
Birmingham through the Magic Lantern
Penzance, Newlyn and the Isles of Scilly
Great Yarmouth through the Magic Lantern
Ancient Baalbec through the Magic Lantern
The Isle of Skye through the Magic Lantern
Ancient Palmyra through the Magic Lantern
The Kentish Coast from Whitstable to Hythe
New South Wales through the Magic Lantern
From Glasgow to Rothesay by paddle steamer
Victorian Childhood through the Magic Lantern
The Way We Were: Yorkshire Railway Stations
Southampton, Portsmouth and the Great Liners
Newcastle upon Tyne through the Magic Lantern
Egypt's Ancient Monuments through the Magic Lantern
The Way We Were: Birkenhead, Port Sunlight and the Wirral
Ancient Egypt, Baalbec and Palmyra through the Magic Lantern

Printed in Great Britain
by Amazon